*The Story of a Special Day*
*Volume 74*

# March 14

73rd day of the year
(74th in leap years)
292 days remaining
until the end of the year.

by Michael Dobson

# Timespinner
# Press

For more information about the series, about us, or about your special day, please email us at editor@timespinnerpress.com.

Look for other volumes in *The Story of a Special Day*, coming often.

# Table of Contents

**Cover:** The symbol for pi (π) over a printout of π to several hundred places, in honor of Pi Day, 3/14.

**Back Cover:** The month of March, from the French Gothic illuminated manuscript *Les Très Riches Heures du duc de Berry.*

# March 14 Quotations

"A superior pilot uses his superior judgment to avoid situations which require the use of his superior skill."

> — *Frank Borman, born March 14, 1928*

"Life is like riding a bicycle. To keep your balance you must keep moving."

> — *Albert Einstein, born March 14, 1897*

"The philosopher have only *interpreted* the world, in various ways. The point, however, is to *change* it."

> — *Karl Marx, died March 14, 1883*

"In this country, it is wise to kill an admiral from time to time to encourage the others."

> — *Voltaire, wrting about the execution of Admiral John Bing on March 14, 1757*

"Whoso pulleth out this sword of this stone and anvil, is rightwise King born of all England."

> — *Sir Thomas Malory, died March 14, 1471*

# Pi Day

The number known as pi (π, 3.14159...) is one of the great curiosities in mathematics. For thousands of year, mathematicians have probed its mysteries and in the proces found literally thousands of uses in geometry, trigonometry, statistics, thermodynamics, mechanics, and electromagnetism. Indeed, π is one of the most useful numbers around.

Pi is an "irrational number," meaning it can't be expressed exactly as the ratio of two numbers. We use approximations such as 22/7, but those aren't exact. When the fraction is represented in decimal numbers, it never ends and never shows a permanent repeating pattern. Pi is also "transcendent," meaning it's not the root of any nonzero polynomial with rational coefficients. That's why the ancient problem of "squaring the circle" with compass and straight-edge is impossible.

Some scholars trace knowledge of π back to ancient Egypt, noting that the Great Pyramid at Giza, constructed somewhere between 2589 and 2566 BCE, has a perimeter of 1760 cubits and a height of 280 cubits, giving it a ratio of about 6.28, or approximately 2π. While this may have been only a coincidence, there is strong evidence that π was known to the Babylonians as early as 1900 BCE, and to the Egyptians no later than 1860 BCE. Sanskrit texts dating back to 600 BC contain approximations of π, and the Bible even mentions a pool in the Temple of Solomon that has measurements approximating π.

The first algorithms for calculating π come from the Greek mathematician Archimedes and the Chinese mathematician Liu Hui (劉徽) in the third century BCE. Many other great mathematicians, including Sir Isaac Newton, worked on the problem of π. Today, computer programs are able to calculate π to over ten trillion digits.

The irrational nature of π has bothered some people in 1897, the Indiana Legislature passed the "Indiana Pi Bill," which claimed a method to square the circle, by establishing the value of π as 3.2. The bill, however, never became law.

Pi is so popular among mathematicians that it has its own holiday, March 14 — 3/14, the first three significant digits of π. Pi Day was first organized by Larry Shaw of the San Francisco Exploratorium in 1988, and in 2009, the U.S. House of representatives recognized National Pi

Day for the first time. On Pi Day, people (naturally) eat pies, and sometimes march in circles.

Because March 14 is also Albert Einstein's birthday, Princeton University, where Einstein worked, has an annual Einstein look-alike contest. The Massachusetts Institute of Technology mails its application decision letters to prospective students on Pi Day at exactly 6.28pm ($2\pi$).

A "Pi" Pie

# March 14 Holidays and Celebrations

## Constitution Day (Andorra)

Andorra, the sixth smallest nation in Europe, is located in the Pyrenees mountains between Spain and France. On March 14, 1993, the Andorran people ratified their constitution in a referendum.

## Heroes Day (St. Vincent and the Grenadines)

Heroes Day in St. Vincent and the Grenadines, a small island nation in the Caribbean, honors Joseph Chatoyer, a Carbi chief who led a revolt against the British colonial government. Chatoyer was killed by British soldiers on March 14, 1795, after leading a long resistance.

## Mother Tongue Day (Estonia)

When the Baltic nation of Estonia was occupied by the Soviet Union in World War II, Estonian became the second language, with Russian as the first. When Estonia regained its independence in

1988, it re-established Estonian as the official language of the country. March 14 is the birthday of Kristjan Jaak Peterson, an Estonian poet considered one of the primary figures of Estonian literature.

## Nanakshahi New Year (ਨਾਨਕਸ਼ਾਹੀ) (Sikhism)

The Nanakshahi calendar (ਨਾਨਕਸ਼ਾਹੀ in Punjabi), is used by adherents of the Sikh religion. The first day of the month of Chet (March 14 in the Gregorian calendar) is the beginning of the year year. It represents the birthday of the first Sikh guru, Nanak Dev (ਗੁਰੂ ਨਾਨਕ) in 1469.

## Second Equirra (Ancient Rome)

The Equirra were the two ancient Roman festival of chariot racing, held in honor of the god Mars. The First Equirra was on February 27, and the Second Equirra on March 14. The races took place on the Campus Martius, the "Field of Mars," on the outskirts of Rome. The Equirra date back to the oldest known Roman calendars.

## Summer Festival (Albania)

The Summer Festival in Albania dates back to pagan times. It celebrates the end of winter, the rebirth of nature, and a rejuvenation of spirt. The celebrations include a marathon and a circus show.

## White Day (ホワイトデ) (Japan, South Korea, Taiwan, and China)

Valentine's Day in certain Asian nations is observed by girls and women, who present gifts of chocolate to boys and men. One month later, on White Day, boys and men return the favor. Typical White Day gifts include cookies, jewelry, white chocolate, white lingerie, and marshmallows. It was first celebrated in 1977 in Japan as "Marshmallow Day" promoted by the confectionery industry.

## Christian Feast Days

Saints commemorated on March 14 include Leobinus and Matilda of Ringelheim.

# What Happened on March 14?

## 1489 CE - Queen Catarina Sells Cyprus

The island nation of Cyprus had fallen under the control of the Mamluk Sultanate of Egypt and Syria in 1426. In 1468 King James II of Cyprus (known as James the Bastard) took a noblewoman of Venice, Catarina Cornaro, as his wife. They married by proxy when Catarina was only 14. James died shortly after the marriage, and their infant son, another James, also died of mysterious circumstances. Venetian merchants gained increasing control over the island, and on March 14, 1489, Queen Catarina was forced to abdicate and sell the country to the Republic of Venice. She kept her title and retired to the Venetian countryside for the rest of her life.

Queen Catarina of Cyprus

# 1757 CE - Execution of Admiral John Byng

The opening battle of the Seven Years' War between France and Great Britian was the Battle of Minorca in 1756. Admiral John Byng was sent to defend Minorca with a fleet of ten ships in poor repair and undermanned, and given little time to prepare. He received a small reinforcement from the Minorcan squadron, but he was still confronted with 12 French ships of the line. Unable to relieve the British garrison at Minorca, and withdrew. Byng was court-martialled for failing to do all he could to fulfill his orders, found guilty, and on March 14, 1757, he was executed by firing squad.

Execution of Admiral Byng

# 1794 CE - Eli Whitney Patents the Cotton Gin

Traditionally, cotton seeds had to be removed from the cotton by hand or by simple seed-removing devices, a labor-intensive task. Eli Whitney developed the modern mechanical cotton gin in 1793, and received his patent on March 14, 1794. The cotton gin made cotton a hugely profitable business and stimulated the textile and machine tool industry in the United States, and had the effect of making slavery even more profitable. Because of this, the cotton gin is often considered one of the root causes of the American Civil War.

# 1885 CE - First Performance of *The Mikado*.

Gilbert and Sullivan's comic opera *The Mikado* opened on March 14, 1885, in London, and ran for 672 performance. Up to that time, it was the longest run for any work of musical theatre. *The Mikado* continues to be extremely popular, performed in amateur and school productions in several languages.

Original publicity poster for *The Mikado*

## 1900 CE - Gold Standard Act

Signed by President William McKinley on March 14, 1900, the Gold Standard Act established gold as the only standard for redeeming paper money, ending "bimetallism," in which silver could be exchanged for gold. The gold standard lasted in American until 1933.

## 1910 CE - Lakeview Gusher

The largest accidental oil spill in history began on March 14, 1910, in Kern County, California, when an attempt to drill into the Midway-Sunset Oil Reserve resulted in a huge blowout, releasing over 9 million barrels of crude oil, more than any single leak on land or water. The site is designated as a California Historical Landmark.

## 1931 CE - First Indian Musical Film

On March 14, 1931, *Alam Ara* (आलम आरा), or *The Ornament of the World*, the first Indian sound film, premiered at the Majestic Cinema in what was then known as Bombay. It was so popular police had to come to control the crowds. A love story with singing, it was the inspiration and template for the Indian film musical (sometimes known as Bollywood) style.

# 1943 CE - Kraków Ghetto Liquidated

Beginning in 1941, the Nazis began forcing Jews in the Podgórize district of occupied Poland into the Kraków Ghetto. Waves of deportations transported thousands of ghetto residents into concentration camps. The final liquidation of the ghetto took place on March 13-14, 1943, when SS troops deported 8,000 Jews to a labor camp, killed 2,000 on the spot, and transported all remaining residents to Auschwitz.

Deportations from the Kraków Ghetto

# 1945 CE - The Grand Slam Bomb

The British "Grand Slam" bomb, also called "Ten Ton Tess," was a 22,000 lb. (10,000 kg) earthquake bomb meant for strategic targets in World War II. It was carried by a specially modified Avro Lancaster bomber. When dropped, the Grand Slam would reach nearly the speed of sound, and penetrate deep underground before exploding, causing an artificial cavern (camouflet) that would undermine the foundation of any large structure nearby. The first Grand Slam bomb was dropped on the Schildesche viaduct, collapsing nearly 100 yards of it. By the end of the war, 42 Grand Slam bombs were dropped.

# 1964 CE - Jack Ruby Found Guilty

On March 14, 1964, a jury in Dallas, Texas, returned a verdict of guilty against Jack Ruby, who killed Lee Harvey Oswald, the sniper who killed John F. Kennedy. Ruby, a nightclub owner in Dallas, died in prison of lung cancer in 1967 while appealing his trial and sentencing.

Jack Ruby about to shoot Lee Harvey Oswald

## 1978 CE - Operation Litani

As a response to the Coastal Road Massacre, which killed 38 Israeli citizens, including 13 children, Israeli forces invaded PLO strongholds in southern Lebanon in what was known as Operation Litani. Begining on March 14, 1978, in a seven-day offensive, Israeli Defense Forces occupied Lebanon up to the Litani River, killing over 1,000 Lebanese and Palestinian civilians, and displacing at least 100,000 from their homes.

## 1995 CE - Soyuz Flies an American

The first American to travel into space on a Russian vehicle was Norman Thagard, who flew on a Soyuz TM-21 spacecraft for the Russian Mir 18 mission. Lifting off from the Baikonur Cosmodrome in Kazakstan on March 14, 1995, the crew landed at Cape Canaveral in the Space Shuttle *Atlantis* on July 7, 1995, after 115 days in space.

# Who Was Born on March 14?

*The abbreviation "O.S." on some dates refers to the fact that the Russian Empire did not switch from the Julian to the Gregorian calendar at the same time as the rest of Europe, and therefore some figures have two dates for their birth or death.*

*People whose original names are not in the Western alphabet have their native names in the appropriate script shown in parenthesis.*

## Acting and Film

### Jamie Bell (March 14, 1986 — )

Jamie Bell's movie roles include Jimmy in the 2005 remake of *King Kong* and the lead character in *The Adventures of Tintin.*

### Liesel Matthews (March 14, 1984 — )

Child actor Liesel Pritzker Simmons, heir to the Hyatt Hotel fortune, starred in 1995's *A Little*

*Princess* and played the President's daughter in *Air Force One* under her stage name.

## Mercedes McNab (March 14, 1980 — )

McNab played Harmony Kendall on *Buffy the Vampire Slayer* and in the spinoff series *Angel*.

## Chris Klein (March 14, 1979 — )

Kris Klein played "Oz" in three of the films in the *American Pie* series.

## Merlin Santana (March 14, 1976 — November 9, 2002)

Santana was Rudy's suitor in *The Cosby Show* and Romeo in *The Steve Harvey Show*. He was shot to death in 2002.

## Daniel Gillies (March 14, 1976 — )

Gillies played Elijah on *The Vampire Diaries*.

## Grace Park (March 14, 1974 — )

Park was on *Battlestar Galactica* and in the remake of *Hawaii Five-0*.

## Meredith Salenger (March 14, 1970 — )

Salenger is known for playing the title role in 1985's *The Journey of Natty Gann*.

## Des Coleman (March 14, 1969 — )

Des Coleman was Lenny in BBC's *EastEnders*.

## Megan Follows (March 14, 1968 — )

Follows played the lead role in the 1985 miniseries *Anne of Green Gables* and sequels.

## Melissa Reeves (March 14, 1967 — )

Reeves played Jennifer Horton on the soap opera *Days of Our Lives* beginning in 1985.

## Gary Anthony Williams (March 14, 1966 — )

Television actor Williams has had ongoing roles in *Weeds, Boston Legal, Malcolm in the Middle*, and other shows as both actor and voice artist.

## Elise Neal (March 14, 1966 — )

Neal is known for her roles in 2005's *Hustle & Flow, seaQuest 2032*, and as Janice on the soap opera *Loving*.

## Amir Khan (March 14, 1965 — )

Bollywood star Khan won his first Filmfare Award for Best Actor in *Raja Hindustani* and was in the Academy Award-nominated *Lagaan*.

## Penny Johnson Jerald (March 14, 1961 — )

Jerald played Beverly on *The Larry Sanders Show*, Kasidy on *Star Trek: Deep Space Nine*, Sherry Palmer on *24*, and Captain "Iron" Gates on *Castle*.

## Gary Dell'Abate (March 14, 1961 — )

Executive producer of *The Howard Stern Show*, Dell'Abate published his autobiography, *They Call Me Baba Booey*, in 2010.

## Tamara Tunie (March 14, 1959 — )

Tunie played Jessica on *As the World Turns*, and the medical examiner on *Law & Order: Special Victims Unit*.

## Billy Crystal (March 14, 1948 — )

Comedian Billy Crystal's first major role was as Jodie on the sitcom *Soap*. He achieved Hollywood stardom in such films as *When Harry Met Sally...* and *City Slickers*, and has hosted the Academy Awards numerous times.

## Steve Kanaly (March 14, 1946 — )

Kanaly is best known as Ray Krebbs from the prime time soap opera *Dallas*.

## Anita Morris (March 14, 1943 — March 2, 1994)

Morris played Danny DeVito's mistress in *Ruthless People* and was in the musical *Nine*.

## Rita Tushingham (March 14, 1942 — )

Tushingham is known for her award-winning role in *A Taste of Honey* and for *The Knack...and How to Get It*.

## Wolfgang Peterson (March 14, 1941 — )

Wolfgang Peterson directed *Das Boot, Enemy Mine, In the Line of Fire, Air Force One,* and other films.

## Michael Caine (March 14, 1933 — )

Michael Caine won two Academy Awards for *Hannah and Her Sisters* and *The Cider House Rules*, and starred in such films as *Zulu, The Ipcress File, Alfie, The Man Who Would Be King, Educating Rita,* and *Dirty Rotten Scoundrels*.

## Doris Eaton Travis (March 14, 1904 — May 11, 2010)

Doris Eaton Travis was the last surviving Ziegfeld girl, and was featured in books and documentaries about the Ziegfeld Follies.

Doris Eaton Travis

# Art

## Diane Arbus (March 14, 1923 — July 26, 1971)

Photographer Diane Arbus is best known for her black and white photographs of "deviant and marginal people."

## Hank Ketcham (March 14, 1920 — June 1, 2001)

Cartoonist Hank Ketcham created *Dennis the Menace.*

### Akira Yoshizawa (吉澤 章) (March 14, 1911 — March 14, 2005)

Yoshizawa, who was born and died on the same day, was known as the grandmaster of origami, creating hundreds of designs shown in diagrams in his 18 books. He was named to the Order of the Rising Sun in Japan.

Akira Yoshizawa with origami

### Adolph Gottlieb (March 14, 1903 — March 4, 1974)

Gottlieb was a leading figure in the American abstract expressionist movement.

# Business

### Jerry Greenfield (March 14, 1951 — )

Greenfield co-founded Ben & Jerry's Ice Cream.

## S. Truett Cathy (March 14, 1921 — )

Cathy founded the fast food restaurant chain Chick-fil-A.

## Philip Vincent (March 14, 1908 — March 27, 1979)

Founder of Vincent Motorcycles, Philip Vincent designed the legendary Vincent Black Shadow and Black Lightning motorcycles.

Vincent Black Shadow motorcycle

# Exploration and Heroism

## Osa Johnson (March 14, 1894 — January 7, 1953)

Adventurer and filmmaker Osa Johnson, with her husband Martin Johnson, wrote I Married Adventure, co-produced *Headhunters of the South Seas, Simba: King of the Beasts,* and others. She hosted *Osa Johnson's The Big Game Hunt*, one of the first TV wildlife series. The couple established a museum in Kansas, and Disney's Animal Kingdom Lodge took its inspiration from their work.

Osa Johnson

## Raoul Lufbery (March 14, 1885 — May 19, 1918)

French-American World War I fighter ace Raoul Lufbery (below) rose to command the legendary Lafayette Escadrille and achieved 16 victories. He died in combat in 1918.

## Casey Jones (March 14, 1863 — April 30, 1900)

Illinois Central railroad engineer Jonathan "Casey" Jones was the sole person killed when his passenger train the *Cannonball Express* collided with a stalled freight train. He was immortalized in "The Ballad of Casey Jones."

# Music

### Taylor Hanson (March 14, 1983 — )

Musician Taylor Hanson is best known as a member of the band Hanson.

### Kristian Bush (March 14, 1970 — )

Bush is known for being a vocalist in the band Sugarland.

### Rick Dees (March 14, 1950 — )

Radio personality Rick Dees is known for the 1976 novelty song "Disco Duck." He has won a People's Choice Award and earned a Grammy nomination, and is in the Broadcast Hall of Fame.

## Walter Parazaider (March 14, 1945 — )

Saxophone player Parazaider is a founding member of the rock group Chicago.

## Michael Martin Murphy (March 14, 1945 — )

Multiple Grammy nominee and country-western singer-songwriter Murphy has had six gold albums and wrote the New Mexico state song.

## Quincy Jones (March 14, 1933 — )

Quincy Jones's career includes 79 Grammy nominations with 27 wins, and a 2013 induction into the Rock & Role Hall of Fame. He produced Michael Jackson's *Thriller* and the charity song "We Are the World."

## Phil Phillips (March 14, 1926 — )

Phillips is best known for his 1959 hit "Sea of Love."

## Les Baxter (March 14, 1922 — January 15, 1996)

Les Baxter conducted the orchestra for Nat King Cole's hit "Mona Lisa," hit #1 with his instrumental version of "Unchained Melody," and wrote the whistle theme from *Lassie*.

## Lee Hays (March 14, 1914 — August 26, 1981)

Hays, a singer with The Weavers, wrote "If I Had a Hammer" and "Kisses Sweeter Than Wine."

## Les Brown (March 14, 1912 — January 4, 2001)

Les Brown and His Band of Renown performed with Bob Hope for nearly 50 years, including 18 USO tours for troops around the world.

## Johann Straus I (March 14, 1804 — September 25, 1849)

Father of "Waltz King" Johann Strauss II, the senior Strauss is best known for the "Radetzky March" as well as for several waltzes of his own.

## Georg Philipp Telemann (March 14, 1681 — June 25, 1767)

German Baroque composer Telemann was one of the most prolific composers in history and author of numerous classical works still performed today.

# Politics and Government

## Albert II, Prince of Monaco (March 14, 1958 — )

Albert II is the son of Prince Ranier III and Grace Kelly, and reigning monarch of the Principality of Monaco.

## Mustafa Barzani (March 14, 1903 — March 1, 1979)

Kurdish nationalist leader Barzani, known as Mullah Mustafa, was the most prominent figure in modern Kurdish politics, leading the Kurdistan Democratic Party in a series of revolutions against Ba'ath rule in Iraq.

## King Umberto I (March 14, 1844 — July 29, 1900)

Known as "the Good," Italian monarch Umberto I was assassinated in 1900.

## King Victor Emmanuel II (March 14, 1820 — January 9, 1878)

Victor Emmanuel II was the first king of a united Italy since the 6th century, and is known as "Father of the Fatherland."

# Science and Space

### Eugene Cernan (March 14, 1934 — )

Astronaut Eugene Cernan was the last man to walk on the moon in the Apollo program. He was pilot of Gemini 9A, lunar module pilot of Apollo 10, and commander of Apollo 17.

Eugene Cernan on the Moon

## Frank Borman (March 14, 1928 — )

Frank Borman commanded Apollo 8 and previously set a space endurance record on Gemini 7.

## Ed Heinemann (March 14, 1908 — November 26, 1991)

Military aircraft designer Ed Heinemann is responsible for the SBD Dauntless, A-20 Havoc, A-26 Invader, A-1 Skyraider, A-3 Skywarrior, F3D Skynight, F4D Skyray, and others. He is in the National Aviation Hall of Fame. The Naval Air Systems Command established the "Edward H. Heinemann Award" for significant contributions to aircraft design.

## Wacław Sierpiński (March 14, 1882 — October 21, 1969)

Polish mathematician Wacław Sierpiński published over 700 papers and 50 books and made contributions to set theory and number theory. Three fractals — the Sierpiński triangle, the Sierpiński carpet, and the Sierpiński curve — and the Sierpiński number are named for him.

## Albert Einstein (March 14, 1879 — April 18, 1955)

Albert Einstein is generally regarded as the father of modern physics and the most influential physicist of the 20th century. He is known for the formula $E=mc^2$ and for the discovery of the photoelectric effect, which won him the 1921 Nobel Prize in Physics.

## Paul Erlich (March 14, 1854 — August 20, 1915)

Physician and medical researcher Paul Erlich popularized the idea of a "magic bullet" against certain diseases and won the 1908 Nobel Prize in Physiology or Medicine for his work in immunology.

## Giovanni Schiaparelli (March 14, 1835 — July 4, 1910)

Italian astronomer Schiparelli's observation of Mars identified a series of linear structures on the surface of the planet, which he called "canali" in Italian, meaning "channels." It was mistranslated into English as "canals," giving rise to the idea (now discredited) of canals — and possibly civilizations — on the Red Planet. Craters on the Moon and Mars are named for him.

## Lucy Hobbs Taylor (March 14, 1833 — October 3, 1910)

Taylor was the first American woman to graduate from dental school and go into practice.

# Sports

## Santino Marella (March 14, 1979 — )

Italian-Canadian wrestler Marella is a former
United States Champion and a two-time
Intercontinental Champion in the WWE.

## Larry Johnson (March 14, 1969 — )

Basketball forward Larry Johnson played for the
Charlotte Hornets and New York Knicks. He was
Rookie of the Year in 1992 in addition to both
college and high school distinctions. He played
on the gold medal winning U.S. basketball teams
in 1994 and 1989. He also appeared on the
sitcom *Family Matters* and as himself in the
movies *Eddie* and *Space Jam*.

## Kiana Tom (March 14, 1965 — )

Fitness expert Kiana Tom hosted *Kiana's Flex
Appeal* on ESPN and wrote *Kiana's Body
Sculpting*. She received the U.S. Sports Academy
Award. She was a cheerleader for the Oakland
Raiders and has appeared on numerous TV
shows.

## Kirby Puckett (March 14, 1960 — March 6, 2006)

Minnesota Twins center fielder Kirby Puckett was the all-time leader in career hits, runs, doubles, and total bases for his franchise, with a career batting average of .318. He was elected to the Baseball Hall of Fame in 2001.

## Wes Unseld (March 14, 1946 — )

Former Washington Bullets star Wes Unseld was inducted into the Naismith Memorial Basketball Hall of Fame in 1988.

## Bob Charles (March 14, 1936 — )

Golfer Bob Charles won 6 PGA tours and 23 Champions tours in a career spanning over 50 years. He was elected to the World Golf Hall of Fame in 2008 and was knighted in 1999.

## William Clay Ford, Sr. (March 14, 1925 — )

Ford, last surviving grandchild of automotive pioneer Henry Ford, owns the Detroit Lions.

## Lee Petty (March 14, 1914 — April 5, 2000)

Legendary NASCAR racer Lee Petty won three Grand National Championships and is in the International Motorsports Hall of Fame.

# Writing

### Kevin Williamson (March 14, 1965 — )

Screenwriter, producer, and director Kevin Williamson is known for the horror films *Scream* and *I Know What You Did Last Summer*, and for the TV series *Dawson's Creek* and *The Vampire Diaries*.

### Tad Williams (March 14, 1957 — )

Tad Williams is a well-known writer of fantasy and science fiction novels.

### Max Shulman (March 14, 1919 — August 28, 1988)

Max Shulman is best remembered for his television and short story character Dobie Gillis. He wrote several best-selling humorous novels, beginning with 1943's *Barefoot Boy With Cheek,* and plays including *The Tender Trap* and *How Now, Dow Jones.*

## Horton Foote (March 14, 1916 — March 4, 2009)

Foote wrote the screenplay for *To Kill a Mockingbird* and received a Pulitzer for his play *The Young Man From Atlanta.* He received the National Medal of Arts, along with two Academy Awards.

## Sylvia Beach (March 14, 1887 — October 5, 1962)

Beach opened the legendary Paris bookstore Shakespeare and Company, which published the first edition of James Joyce's *Ulysses* in 1922.

## Algernon Blackwood (March 14, 1869 — December 10, 1951)

English short story writer Algernon Blackwood is remembered for his ghost stories and other weird/horror fiction.

## Arthur O'Shaughnessy (March 14, 1844 — January 30, 1881)

Poet Arthur O'Shaughnessy is famous for the line "We are the music makers/and we are the dreamers of dreams," which has been used in such works as *Willy Wonka & the Chocolate Factory*, the motivational speech given before the U.S. hockey team beat Russia in the 1980 Olympics, and in numerous songs.

## Charles Cutter (March 14, 1837 — September 6, 1903)

Librarian Charles Cutter developed the "Cutter number" system, still used today in libraries. He is a member of the Library Hall of Fame.

# Who Died on March 14?

## Acting and Film

### Peter Graves (March 18, 1926 — March 14, 2010)

Peter Graves was best known for his starring role in the television series *Mission: Impossible*. He was the younger brother of actor James Arness.

Peter Graves (right) and the *Mission: Impossible* 5th season cast

## Gareth Hunt (February 7, 1942 — March 14, 2007)

Hunt was known for playing Frederick the footman in *Upstairs, Downstairs*, and for his role in the *New Avengers* television series.

## Kirk Alyn (October 8, 1910 — March 14, 1999)

Alyn was the first actor to play Superman on screen in a 1948 film serial.

## Fred Zinnemann (April 29, 1907 — March 14, 1997)

Zinnemann won Academy Awards as Best Director for *From Here to Eternity* and *A Man for All Seasons*.

# Animals

## Balto (1919— March 14, 1933)

Siberian Husky sled dog Balto led the team on the final leg of the 1925 journey to deliver diphtheria antitoxin to the isolated community of Nome. The Iditarod Trail Sled Dog Race commemorates the run.

# Art

## Chic Young (January 9, 1901— March 14, 1973)

Chic Young created the long-running comic strip *Blondie,* which had a peak readership of 52 million.

Cast of the *Blondie* comic strip

## Jacob Isaakszoon van Ruisdael (c. 1628 — March 14, 1682)

Van Ruisdael was a Dutch Golden Age painter of landscapes.

*View of Bentheim Castle* by Jacob van Ruisdael

# Music and Dance

### Doc Pomus (June 27, 1925 — March 14, 1991)

Under his stage name, Jerome Felder was the lyricist behind such hits as "A Teenager in Love," "Save the Last Dance for Me," "This Magic Moment," and many others.

## Howard Ashman (May 5, 1950 — March 14, 1991)

Ashman collaborated with Alan Menkin on several Disney films including *The Little Mermaid, Beauty and the Beast*, and *Aladdin.*

## Busby Berkeley (November 29, 1895 — March 14, 1976)

Acclaimed choreographer and movie director Busby Berkeley was known for his elaborate musical production numbers.

Busby Berkeley number from *42nd Street*

## Susan Hayward (June 30, 1917 — March 14, 1975)

Actress Susan Hayward was nominated for five Academy Awards, winning one. Her films include *The President's Lady, I'll Cry Tomorrow,* and *I Want to Live!*

# Politics

## Karl Marx (May 5, 1818 — March 14, 1883)

Economist and political philosopher Karl Marx was the developer of communism, often referred to as Marxism.

Karl Marx

# Science and Invention

## William Fowler (August 9, 1911 — March 14, 1995)

Astrophysicist Willy Fowler won the 1983 Nobel Prize for explaining the abundance of heavier chemical elements in the process of nucleosynthesis. He is one of the authors of the landmark study known to astrophysicists as $B^2FH$.

## Howard H. Aiken (March 8, 1900 — March 14, 1973)

Computer pioneer Howard Aiken was the conceptual designer of the pioneering IBM Harvard Mark I computer.

## George Eastman (July 12, 1854— March 14, 1932)

Eastman founded the Eastman Kodak Company and invented roll film.

# Sports

## Ann Calvello (August 1, 1929 — March 14, 2006)

Roller derby star Ann Calvello, nicknamed "Banana-Nose" for having her nose broken 12 times in her career, was inducted into the Roller Derby Hall of Fame in 1968. She was the subject of the 2001 documentary *Demon of the Derby.*

## Happy Humphrey (July 16, 1926 — March 14, 1989)

Professional wrestler William Cobb billed himself as "the world's largest wrestler," with weight fluctuating between 750 and 800 pounds.

## Marion Jones (Farquhar) (November 2, 1879 — March 14, 1965)

Tennis player Marion Jones won the women's singles titles at the 1899 and 1902 U.S. Championships, and is in the International Tennis Hall of Fame.

Marion Jones Farquhar

### Oliver Kirk (April 20, 1884 — March 14, 1960)

Kirk won two gold medals in boxing at the 1904 Summer Olympics, and is the only boxer in Olympic history to win gold in two separate weight divisions (bantamweight and featherweight) at the same Olympics.

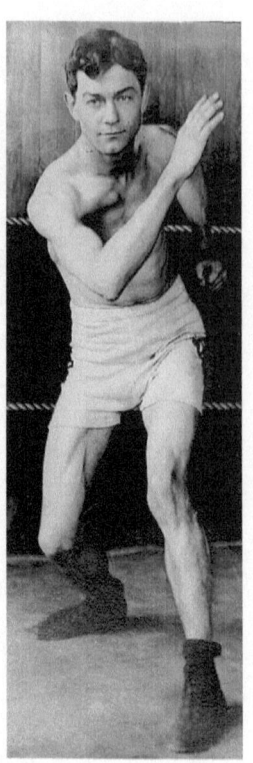

Oliver Kirk

# Writing

### Cherry Wilder (September 3, 1930 — March 14, 2002)

New Zealand author Cherry Lockett Grimm published over 50 science fiction short stories and novels under the name Cherry Wilder.

## Jean Poiret (August 17, 1926 — March 14, 1992)

Actor, director, and screenwriter Jean Poiret is best known as the author of the original play *La Cage Aux Folles*.

## Margery Sharp (January 25, 1905— March 14, 1991)

Sharp's best known work is *The Rescuers*, a children's book series adapted into two Disney films.

## Edward Abbey (January 29, 1927 — March 14, 1989)

Environmental activist Edward Abbey, described as the "Thoreau of the American West," wrote the novel *The Monkey Wrench Gang*, cited as an inspiration by radical environmental groups.

## Sir Thomas Malory (c. 1405 — March 14, 1471)

Malory is known as the author or compiler of *Le Morte d'Arthur*, the story of King Arthur.

An illustration by Aubrey Beardsley from *Le Morte d'Arthur*

# March: The Third Month

In ancient Rome, March was the first month of the year. As the first month of spring, in the Mediterranean climate it marked the beginning of the military campaign season. That's why March (Martius) is named in honor of Mars, the Roman god of war.

Although the first month of the year was moved back to January sometime during the transition of Rome from a kingdom to a republic (historians differ), March was the first month of the year in Russia until the end of the 15th Century, and is the first month of the year in many other cultures and religions.

In the northern hemisphere, March 1 marks the beginning of meteorological spring. In the southern hemisphere, March is the equivalent of September, making southern hemisphere March the beginning of autumn.

March is one of the seven months that have 31 days in it. March starts on the same day of the week as November every year, and except for leap years starts on the same day as February. March starts on the same day of the week as the previous June except for leap years, and in leap years starts on the same day as the previous September and December.

## March in Other Cultures

In Finland, March is called *maaliskuu* (earthy month). In Ukraine, it's *березень* (birch tree). Other names for March include *Lentmonat* (Saxon), *Hyld-monath* (Angles), and *sušec* (Slovene).

## March Symbols

**Birthstones:** Aquamarine and bloodstone, both representing courage.

Aquamarine

# Birth Flowers: Daffodils

Daffodils in Bagatelle Park, Paris, France

The month of March, from the illuminated manuscript *Les Très Riches Heures du duc de Berry*

# March Events

**Honorary months:** Presidents, Congresses, and nations around the world issue proclamations recognizing particular months to honor certain causes. These events generally fall in March. (All US unless otherwise noted.)

- National Nutrition Month

- American Red Cross Month

- Women's History Month (celebrated in Canada during October)

- Irish-American Heritage Month

- Colorectal Cancer Awareness Month

- Fire Prevention Month (The Philippines)

**"March Madness":** (United States) The NCAA Men's Division I Basketball Championship, popularly known as "March Madness" or the "Big Dance," is a single-elimination tournament to establish the champion college basketball team.

**Multi-day events:** Some March events span multiple days.

- **Nineteen Day Fast:** (Bahá'í Faith) March 2 through March 20

- **Girl Scout Week:** (U.S.) The week that includes March 12, the date of the founding of the first chapter of the Girl Scouts of the USA in 1912. The earliest Girl Scout Week can start is March 6, and the latest it can end is March 18. The Sunday of Girl Scout Week is celebrated by some churches as Girl Scout Sunday or Girl Scout Sabbath.

**Movable events:** Some events change dates from year to year.

- **Commonwealth Day:** Commonwealth Day, formerly Empire Day, celebrates the establishment of the Commonwealth of Nations. It is marked by a service in Westminster Abbey and by a speech by England's monarch to the Commonwealth nations around the world. Commonwealth Day is held annually on the second Monday in March, which can fall on any day between March 8 and March 14.

- **Canberra Day:** In the Australian Capital Territory, Canberra Day celebrates the official naming of Australia's capital city. It is also held annually on the second Monday in March.

- **Passion Sunday:** The fifth Sunday of the Christian season of Lent is known as Passion Sunday in various Protestant denominations and by some traditionalist Catholics. Sometimes, the sixth Sunday of Lent is also known as Passion Sunday, but it is more commonly known as Palm Sunday. Passion Sunday starts the two week Passiontide, which ends on Holy Saturday, the day before Easter, commemorating the day that Jesus's body was laid in the tomb. The fifth Sunday of Lent can occur as early as March 8, and as late as April 11.

# March Zodiac Signs

From the perspective of someone on Earth, the Sun appears to move through the sky throughout the year, along a path astronomers call the ecliptic plane. The ecliptic plane is divided into twelve constellations, known as the zodiac, based on traditionally observed patterns of stars. On your birthday, you can't see your constellation, because it's part of the daytime sky.

The zodiac was first developed by Babylonian astronomers about 2,500 years ago. Because they were unaware that the Earth wobbles like a spinning top (a motion known as precession), they didn't make allowance for the fact that the Sun's path through the zodiac changes over time. That means there are now two sets of dates for your birth sign. The tropical dates are the original Babylonian dates; the siderial dates tell you where the Sun actually appears as it moves along its annual path.

March 14 is in Pisces in tropical dates, and is in Aquarius in siderial.

# Aquarius

**Tropical** January 20 to February 19

**Siderial** February 12 to March 14

Aquarius is one of the oldest recognized constellations, originally representing the Babylonian god Ea. In Latin, Aquarius means "water-carrier," represented in its symbol. In Greek mythology, Aquarius is sometimes associated with Deucalion, who survived a world-cleansing flood. In Chinese astronomy, it is known as the Black Tortoise of the North (北方 玄武, Běi Fāng Xuán Wǔ).

In astrology, Aquarius is considered to be masculine and extroverted, and despite the name is an air sign. Aquarians are supposed to be philanthropical, inventive, and individualistic.

# Pisces

**Tropical** February 20 to March 20

**Siderial** March 15 to April 14

In the Roman legend of Venus and her son Cupid, they escaped the clutches of Typhon, known as the "father of all monsters," by transforming into fish and tying themselves together with rope. That's why the name Pisces is plural for fish. The constellation appears as a somewhat ragged "V" shape, representing the rope, with the "fish" located at the two rope ends.

In astrology, Pisces is a water sign, compatible with the other water signs Cancer and Scorpio, as well as with the earth signs Taurus, Virgo, and Capricorn. Pisceans are supposed to be imaginative, compassionate, unworldly, secretive, and escapist.

# What Day of the Week is March 14?

On what day of the week does March 14 fall?

Surprisingly, this isn't an easy question. Because the calendar year is 365 days long (366 in leap years), it doesn't divide evenly by the seven days of the week.

Also, the Earth goes around the Sun in about 365-1/4 days, so a calendar tends to drift over time. That's why the same date falls on different weekdays in different years.

This is made even more complicated by a change in calendars that took place in 1582. Our modern calendar has its roots in ancient Rome, in a calendar reform conducted by Julius Caesar. Caesar commissioned mathematicians to attack the problem, and came up with the idea of *leap years,* and thus standardized the calendar for centuries to come. This was called the *Julian calendar.*

Over time, however, the small errors in Caesar's calculation compounded. That's why Pope Gregory XIII commissioned the *Gregorian calendar,* used in most of the world today. Some countries converted in 1582, when the calendar was first developed; some converted later; other still haven't changed.

Gregorian and Julian aren't the only types of calendars. The Hebrew year, the Islamic year, and many other calendars are used in different parts of the world and among different people.

You can convert Gregorian dates to other calendars, including the Hebrew calendar, the Islamic calendar, and even the Mayan calendar by visiting the Fourmilab Calendar Converter at http://www.fourmilab.ch/documents/calendar/.

A 50-year brass perpetual calendar.

# Copyright, Credit, and Contact

## Follow Us

Our blog Dobson's Improbable History features short articles on events and people associated with each day, and updates several times each week. Get the latest on Twitter @SidewiseThinker.

## Sources and Art Credits

All art and photographs are either in the public domain or used under a Creative Commons license. Attribution is provided where requested by the copyright owner or when of historical significance, listed below.

- The cherry "pi" pie was photographed by Dan Sheadel and is used here under the Creative Commons Attribution-Share Alike 2.0 Generic license.

- The portrait of Queen Caterina of Cyprus by Gentile Bellini is in the public domain because its copyright has expired. The original can be seen at the Budapest Museum of Fine Arts.

- The *Shooting of Admiral Byng* is an engraving in the collection of the National Portrait Gallery. It is in the public domain because its copyright has expired.

- The 1919 D'Oyly Carte Opera Company publicity poster for *The Mikado* was illustrated by J. Hassal. It is in the public domain because its copyright has expired.

- The photograph of Jews being deported from the Kraków Ghetto is from Istytut Pamieci Narodowej by way of the United States Holocaust Memorial Museum and is in the public domain in both Poland and the United States.

- The photograph of Jack Ruby about to shoot Lee Harvey Oswald was taken on November 24, 1963 by Jack Beers, Jr., a photographer with the Dallas Morning News. It is in the public domain because its copyright was not renewed.

- The photograph of Doris Eaton Travis as a Ziegfield girl is in the public domain because its copyright has expired.

- The illustration of *Dennis the Menace* by Hank Ketcham is covered by copyright, but its use here is covered by U. S. fair use laws because it illustrates an educational article about the entity it represents, is used as the primary visual identification of the topic, is of low resolution and not suitable for the publication of counterfeit goods, is not used in such a way as to suggest to a reader that the use is authorized, and is not replaceable with an uncopyrighted image of comparable educational value.

- The painting *View of Bentheim Castle* by Jacob Isaakszoon van Ruisdael is in the Royal Picture Gallery Maritshuis in The Hague. It is in the public domain because its copyright has expired.

- The screen capture of a Busby Berkeley number from the trailer for the 1933 Warner Brothers film *42nd Street* is in the public domain.

- The portrait of Karl Marx is from the International Institute of Social History in Amsterdam. It is in the public domain because its copyright has expired.

- The 1900 photograph of Marion Jones Farquhar is in the public domain because its copyright has expired.

- The 1910 photograph of boxer Oliver Kirk is from the Library of Congress Prints and Photographs Division. It is in the public domain because its copyright has expired.

- The drawing "How Sir Bedivere Cast the Sword Excalibur into the Water," from the 1894 edition of *Le Morte d'Arthur* by Sir Thomas Malory, is in the public domain because its copyright has expired.

- The illustration of the month of March used on the back cover and in the interior is from the French Gothic illuminated manuscript *Les Très Riches Heures du duc de Berry* by the Limbourg Brothers, Jean Colombe, and an intermediate painter whose name is lost to history. It is in the public domain because its copyright has expired.

- The photograph of aquamarine has been released into the public domain.

Timespinner
Press